Pictures in the Firestorm

SECOND EDITION, REVISED

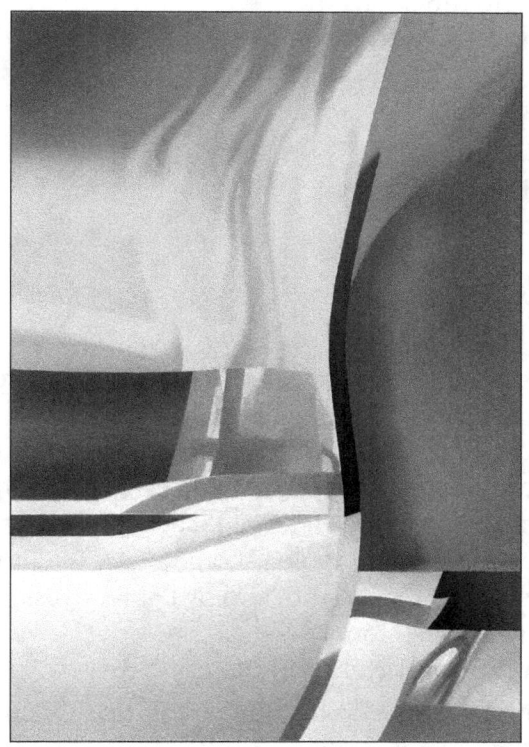

Lauren Rusk

Plain View Press   www.plainviewpress.net
1101 W. 34th Street, STE 404, Austin, TX 78705

Copyright © 2015 Lauren Rusk. All rights reserved under International and Pan-American Copyright Conventions. No part of this book may be reproduced or distributed in any form or by any means, or stored in a data base or retrieval system, without written permission from the author. All rights, including electronic, are reserved by the author and publisher.

ISBN: 978-1-63210-016-0
Library of Congress Control Number: 2015945781

Cover illustration by Tina Tatai.

Acknowledgments

Many of the poems have appeared, some in earlier versions, in the following journals and anthologies: *American Poetry Journal*, *Best New Poets*, *Café Review*, *Cloud View Poets*, *Fire* (UK), *Forty-Three* (UK), *Gathered: Contemporary Quaker Poets*, *The Interpreter's House* (UK), *The Pharos*, *Poor Yorick Journal*, *Saint Elizabeth Street*, *Sand Hill Review*, and *Sequoia*. "Anthropologist on Venus" is reprinted from *The Pharos*, summer 2006. Copyright 2006 by Lauren Rusk. By permission of Alpha Omega Alpha Honor Medical Society. "Sewing Machine" is reprinted from the *American Poetry Journal*, 3:1.

"Adrift at Notre Dame" won one of the two Open Competition Prizes awarded for poems in *Best New Poets 2005*.

I am grateful to those who contributed to the genesis and improvement of this book: Marvin Bell, Susan Bright, Lora Change, Carol Creedon, Mary Crow, W. S. Di Piero, Sheila Donohue, Lynn Emanuel, Jody Gladding, Jorie Graham, Kelvin Gregory, Kenneth Hanson, Joan Houlihan, Al Jacobs, Pam Knight, Marion Knox, Kelly Lenox, Annie Lighthart, Paul Merchant, LouAnn Muhm, William Olsen, Mary Ruefle, Natasha Sajé, David St. John, Lisa Steinman, Leslie Ullman, John Vergin, Nance Van Winckel, Rhett Watts, Roger Weingarten, and especially Eric Roberts, Mark Doty, and Betsy Sholl.

To Eric, with love

Contents

Acknowledgments	2

I

Face to Face with Flags	11
Sight Unseen	13
Women, Windows	17
Adrift at Notre Dame	18
Making a Scene	22
Theater in the Round	26
Fugitive, 1968	28
The Woman with Pots on Her Belt	33
Art Happens	34
Ode to a Bone	39
Unentitled	40

II

The Upstairs Room	45
Happy Donuts	46
On My Own	50
Jet Lagged in Oxford	51
The Stanford Quad as Evening Falls	52
Coming Up with Questions	53
Anthropologist on Venus	54
At the Corner Table	55
Building Down	56
Presence	58
Sewing Machine	59
After the Ice Storm	60
The Village Printing Shop	62
At the Holocaust Museum	63
Grace among the Cacti	67

Behind the Windshield, 2003	70
Pictures in the Firestorm	71
Perhaps a Glimpse	77
Notes	81
About the Author	83

Pictures in the Firestorm

SECOND EDITION, REVISED

I

Face to Face with Flags

Without a sill, I could step right into blue Nevada
from room 301, the faraway clouds
by painters ignoring one another—
chiaroscuro mounds ruled straight across the bottom,
single strokes wisping out on their own,
a childish sheep—but mostly blue, wide
blue,

against which gesticulate
a pair of flags, just outside
the window.

Both face the same way, like horses' heads
sniffing the breeze, listening to something I can't hear.

The nose lifts,
                crumples,
falls—
        I would not give a boy a flag
                              to carry over a hill.

But look—waves of lilies,
                the fluidest
conductor's hands—
        glissando, switch and snap!

A dumbshow,
        these simple
tethered scraps,
        with two corners free.
                          They catch—

stanza break

translate—the merest nuance,
                              the invisible,
    stateless air.

Sight Unseen
   Santa Fe, New Mexico

1.

I came to see the conquistador, bronze
Oñate, who meant to have the last word
against a tribe of Ácoma rebels:

Cut the right foot off
each able-bodied man.
The other will remind them
they should have yielded
their winter corn,
not forced us to take it
at such cost—my nephew!
Now they'll serve—
their women, their godless
old and small.

The story lasts in the dust.
It rises and goes on,

as in the Native museum
it propelled me back outside

to look for a recent sculpture of Oñate,
ruler of Nuevo México, the newly named
colony, exalted

on a horse again, not far
from the Ácoma.

2.

That which happened continues,
a tale told in quiet, from one to another.

A few friends at night,
ordinary Indian men, take turns
with a hacksaw. Their resounding
understatement. A bronze boot

does not appall the stars.

3.

A Laguna woman on the road
drew me a map to Alcalde,
where I drove to see the statue
with its foot hacked off.

Perhaps she thought I knew
the officials had replaced it
with a fresh extremity;

a blowtorch had erased the seam,
though not the history,
which sparkles and rises like mineral dust
as bronze goes dark.

4.

When I arrived the Oñate Center was closed,
a chain across the driveway for Memorial Day.
Scrambling under, I tripped,
scraping the heels of my hands,
stooping and stumbling, grateful
for the impromptu ritual.

5.

There it was—unexpectedly compelling,
not stiff and blank, but spirited—
the big-nosed European visage full of thought
(later I read it wasn't Oñate's face),
the stallion's body pulsing, his knee lifted
by a whole system of sinews,
the back hoof pushing off,
the caverns of his nostrils sucking in the sky.

6.

The best vantage point is just below
the small hill the pedestal surmounts,
where Juan de Oñate looks down on,
but not at, you.

From this angle, both boots are visible—outsized,
with sharp toes and, most of all,
the spurs, one too close
to the stallion's flank, the other,
as I look up,   *stanza break*

a wheel of spikes
against the unremitting sky,
a forged thing
attempting to say, *I am the sun.*

Women, Windows
after Vermeer

Light on a wall,
a woman. Light—

the pour of milk, her round

forehead as she reads

where he arranged her—each
of those women—

near a window to catch the glow,
not look through.

But to the women that light means
opening out—

bellying clouds

painted on the virginals
she's poised to play,

a stretch of river blowing—

lifting her pen, she pauses—

tuning a lute string,

listens—does it
ring true?

The seeds prick and sparkle like water,
in her cracked wheat

rising on the sill.

Adrift at Notre Dame

1.

The organ resounds within   this hollow mountain,
chaos rolls forth,
             the hand of creation
works upon the darkness,
                  rumbling my chest,
the instrument's   instrument.

Here so soon after
             enfolding silence,
familiar though Parisian,
              the Quaker meeting
where I dozed, then   flailed awake

to noon to stumble
             into all this . . .
                     folderol,
I would have said.

2.

French burbles from the pulpit,
                easy to ignore
when you get only scraps,
            except *"Le Seigneur"* . . .

But I didn't come to cavil
             at *les masculins et féminins,*
rather, to feel
        what I can.

3.

The priest looks kindly
                          in my direction
as though at a grandchild.
                               I hear
"*vous imaginez*" . . .
                    "*mystère*" . . .
"*aimer*," to love;
                why not

give up this problem of belief?
                               Just feel—

but through the senses   there's the rub.

For me, the spirit stirs
                      in the trees,
in a painting,
          in a face—

an old Quaker woman's
                    furrowed peace.

Maybe even here—
                 the glass-struck light,
these greens and blues,

      gold and scarlet fashioned into . . .

Now he's angry.
                The finger jabs:
"*impératifs du papa*."

                                                          two-line break

But then, "*Enfin,*"
      the congregants turn
and give one another
      "*la paix,*"
the handshake,
    touch
what is, what is not.

4.

Around the vast perimeter,
altars, alcoves—one unlit,
a jumble of storage
we're supposed to glide by.

A single stone tenant
reclines on a dais,
as they seem often to do.
Some understanding has come to him.

He lifts a gentle hand to tell it
  to the chairs,
   the scaffolding and coils of wire,
the foolish bubble wrap
      foaming from its box,
the vacuum machine . . .

5.

A donkey pokes his nose out
from a frieze called *Le mystère
de l'humanité du Christ*.
Providing the flight from Egypt,
he gazes at me abstractedly,
ears pricked as if he hears—
what? and wonders why he's there.
Among many gospel figures
the donkey stands out, his head
the highest relief.
I love
his obscurity,
the way he loiters
in the now,
his sensitive muzzle
inviting—though it's not permitted—
touch.

Making a Scene

                Caught me off guard—his sudden
handshake—
        I'm Andre Braugher,
I'll be in your section—
                the smile with which
he foiled the random

              parceling out of students
 among teaching assistants, to pick me!
                    (Though I'd hoped
his challenging questions,
which made even the professor
pause, would fall to the lot
of a more seasoned TA.
      Maybe he observed my own
habit of seeking gaps
in the lectures, jumping in . . .)

And now, he's up there—
              taking the chance for extra credit
   in front of the whole class,
   the TAs, Dr. Rebholz—
          up on that hulking counter
              with a washbasin to look out for!

  (How could they—Shakespeare,
   for heaven's sake—in this arena
   for the sciences, experiments . . .)

        Standing there, legs apart.

two-line break

Too young, at twenty,
         for Mark Antony
                astride the world and sinking . . .

  Too   black—no,
                that's not it,

except—his teeshirt, white,
                insists
his body
     raises the stakes.

    Refusing to wear a costume, that too
jacks up the ante.
          He concedes nothing—
not the black
      plastic glasses strapped
around his shaved head,
          nothing except
now a sword-shaped
         piece of cardboard—
   why—

     our breath, a well . . .

from which he draws up

this Roman
renegade,
     coursing with October's life,
                 even as
he struggles to end it,
      his breast opposing

 the blade—
    Did tears
blur us all?
    I know this much:
        there was
        no sound
but his toppling—
    Seal then!

No—he stumbles
   to one knee,
calling, *Eros!*

who would rather slay himself,
       it befalls,
than his captain.

Antony, steeled thus
to impale himself as well,
   yet veers
     (by luck, by inclination)
  from the heart

and is borne, dying
  to his Egypt,
who only feigned her death

to call him back
   to his senses,
  us to ours . . .

          two-line break

but I've left Andre out—
as he does,
yet he's there—

magnifying chance by choice:

Antony in the flesh.

Theater in the Round

Like brown leaves blown, they drift
across the moonlit pond, the ducks
awakened by a sense of manna
flung from a napkin

because I want to stir, a bit,
the balm of water, trees, air.
Sotto voce, quack quack.

Patrons, I and my drowsy consort
linger after Shakespeare,
the lovely park to ourselves.

Then—is't a trick o' th' night?

Or swans, a pair?
Elliptical white shadows
farther out against the dark.

One seems—does it?—
to change shape, unfold,
exploding in slow motion.

Swandragon. See-through.

Doubting sight, I hear . . .
sheets snapping on the line,
or, yes, bellying wings!
Now I see—what

a show! The mute swan
snakes his throat—
for us! And yet

stanza break

these royals, I've heard,
never play to the crowd,
and accept gifts only at dawn.

Oh heavens, he means, Clear out!

You've rumpled the water, agitated
my subjects with your crumbs.
Wasn't *Hamlet* turbulent enough?

We've created a spectacle, the swan and I—
his majesty, my power—
each of us demanding, Why

must it always be about you?

Fugitive, 1968

Fleeing, escaping.
Moving from place to place.
Hard to grasp or retain, as in "a fugitive relationship."
Likely to change, fade, or disappear, as in "a fugitive pigment."

Life seemed to begin at Woolworth's
in the middle of San Francisco,
the farthest we could travel
by Greyhound from Fort Bliss—
the dun green clods
who wanted to break us apart
with their metal instruments,
who couldn't make you hold a gun.

Strange, when we wouldn't let go
of each other, they called it "deserting"
on your part, "harboring" on mine.

Welded by duress
like two sides of a coin,
we went spinning away

to the biggest dime store I'd ever seen—
miles of far-fetched tins: toffee, oolong, kumquats;
tiers of nail polish, a cheering stadium;
and the fabric, dollar-a-yard! I billowed
like a Rossetti absently through the crowd,
nearly nude under the soft corduroy,
rapt and freed among the folds.

Making myself was so much
mixed together with you.

stanza break

Being loved made me pale,
primed for your more subtle palette,
though you loved me first
with India ink under my nails, laughing,
you said, at the fools all around us.

Remember the main entrance? That clanging corner
where the cable car pivots
on the brink of crossing trolleys,
and Haré Krishnas kept up their hopping din
across from the Salvation Army band?
People flocking in were always startled and looked past
the big man with no legs
on a platform of boards and roller-skate wheels,
who had, at a glance, a disdainful mouth.
And the hellfire codger,
if he went for a bag of jellybeans,
his vacated sandwich board stood on its own;
who would bother the flame-staggered letters,
dumbly pronouncing?

But then, who were we
to pronounce others foolish,
you and I in the midst of all this,
going on about the fin de siècle,
taking sides?

I began to cultivate humility
in a knock-wood sort of way,
to be an example,
so nothing would ever change.
An example to you—I'm sorry—
though I loved you first
as I found you.

stanza break

("Trees aren't green, they're blues and yellows.
Brown is really white," you said,
glorying in not explaining.)

Did I tell you why I made clothes
that would look just as graceful
on an old woman?
So we'd always be together.

Got rid of those fishnet tights.
I know you loved them,
but they waffled my ass,
when everything had to be perfect.

Soon even the ocean wind,
my intimate, propelling spirit,
became a wall to push back
with every step. I braced myself
against buffets and bursts. But you,

my teacup-collector,
you weren't afraid of surprises.
You disappeared. Then came back.
"Omelets with Vincent Price," you said.
"He had a flat tire, and I lent him five dollars."

After all, anything might happen in San Francisco,
and who could lie to me, who loved—
I was wingéd victory, wasn't I?
And down the street, "Long Distance."

The switchboard shone black
at work, a gleaming night
with moving, recurring stars.

I plugged out their lights,
and wrapped together voices
through the dark.

We were hiding
in all these convergences—
from ordinariness,
hiding on the unparalleled streets
slanting down like rays rebounding
back from death.

In the five-and-dime lottery,
remember how you tried to win
the old poodle they couldn't sell?
I never thought we'd get a canary,
but Gaylord was the loveliest
apricot and brown. And he did sing,
whenever the water was running.

We had to take the escalator down
to ferns, fish, and Fruit of the Loom,
men's underpants, new to me,
so matter-of-factly white—
each endowed with a school-prize sticker:
grapes, apples, pears . . .

In the heart of the store by the unrolling escalator,
we had each other by the hand;

past the gadget seller's carrot-rasping claims,
we turned to go down (remember?)
when I stopped, mesmerized
by orchids hung against the chrome,

stanza break

each stem held by a crystal test tube,
clear in its finger of water,
each petal curving at different angles,
the singular blossoms
unharmed, magenta and cream.

The Woman with Pots on Her Belt

bristles beside me in memory
like a crowder at a museum,
usurping my view.
She was not, I think, homeless

that time we converged
at the bus stop, but solitary
amid the commuters—
rigged out like a prospector,

her jeans and vest, pots and pans,
ready for what? Apparently not
for a braless young bohemian
in full sail on the corner.

Why did she keep on glaring?
Did she find me too big, too naked,
was I the odd one, after all?

Maybe she willed me not to smirk
at her clanking hips. (I did,
telegraphing, "I'm not her.")

Or could she perhaps have sensed
the cloak of new love,
that scratchy warmth I wore?

Loved or unloved,
when does one begin to think,

 "Of course,
it's what I deserve"?

Art Happens

The wall: smeared
with swirls of shit . . . and I
had to be the one
of all the preschool teachers
to discover it. All
I could think was enforce
the rule: clean it all up.
—Louisa!

"What did you do in the block room?"
"I didn't do it."—Aha,
knowledge of the crime!—
"The big blue whale did it,
and he's a boy." Clearly
only a boy could so disgust,
only a whale so overwhelm.
I, pointing dramatically down:
"You're the whale,
and you did it."
She, spiking out her elbows:
"So?"

Louisa, at the wrong end of the spyglass . . .
how you take your cue!

We play it out:
the delinquent marshaled off
to restore the wall.
I demonstrate the sponge,
the different buckets,
then sit emphatically
on a tiny chair,

breathing through my mouth.
Louisa scours in circles
with myopic concentration . . .
making small windows
in the brown. She's all taken up
with the sopping
and the torque
of wringing out, the ochre
to white of it. I only want
the whole thing done
before the others find out.

Too appalled to ask
how the mural came about.
What slap-prints . . . swipes,
what tendrils,

      what vortices?

And what camaraderie?
Neither of us mentions
her accomplice.

No real talk, just
"You missed some, over there."
And yet, a certain
companionship.
She scrubs. I sit.
Without raging,
              or leaving.
Not telling,
          not touching—
Louisa isn't a child you can touch.

stanza break

Her eyes dazzle when you speak—
staring, unfocused—who knows
how light breaks?

Once, on playhouse pillows
she lolls like a zombie
as I read *Best Friends*
aloud, to the air.
Suddenly she shouts, "Willow—
she's my friend!" Breathless.
"Willow laughs at my jokes!
Every day I wait for her."
Who wouldn't,
for that rose and flax
collapse of giggles?
Nothing like Louisa,
wispy, wrung.

Only now do I picture—
though I saw them whispering
before the fact—a rosy apprentice
dabbing the wall.
Hiccuping with delight,
she mimics the maestro's sweep.
A symphony in brown, once only,
the wallboard shining through.

How I love you
in retrospect, Louisa.

Every eight o'clock
she finds her way
into the giant room. Sometimes
she teeters in the doorframe,
grinning to be seen,
the ironed smell of cotton

rising from her chest. Others,
she edges through,
vague and tough,
yesterday's dress, grit
between her toes.

Itchy, scratchy Louisa,
skulking round the cubbies.

Emerging in a fuchsia sweater,
shiny-buckled mary-janes,
and, I seem to remember,
a rhinestone tiara.
"No—they're *mine* . . .
I found them!"
Robbed, Louisa
scorns her grimy thongs.

Shrugging off large hands one day,
she heads for magazines to tear
and lots of glue,
at a table barely watched
by one abstracted grownup.
While other children simply
paste and wander off,
Louisa builds collage after collage
that tells no story
but its own making, the meditation
of her gluey fingers.

As soon as she surrenders one, sagging
on its heavy paper,
she slathers and crumples again,
smoothes and pats,

until she's made so many
they pile up on the shelf.

At closing time, the child runs
to claim her creations.
Oh, but they're all stuck together,
and those who try to ease
one from another
rip them terribly.

No holding her
can restore that pulpy splendor.
No wonder
Louisa cries, the only time,
with hoarse, adult grief.

Earlier, I saw the teacher's aide
stack the damp collages
and worried, but walked by.

Small self no one knows
what to do with,

how gropingly now

      I work you back
through the pages,

            sticky Louisa.

Ode to a Bone

Long and slender, perhaps a bird's,
one side driftwood,
smooth and bleached,
the other scuzzy
with fiber and dirt,

it balances lightly
between my fingers,
a spoon without a bowl,
the handle-end a ball
that skipped out on its socket.

A truant, my treasure,
spoon-pen,
word-bone
What will you feed me?
What have you spilt?

Once, I suppose, you beat the air,
laboring to soar,
to keep your feathercraft
aloft,
pen-bone, air-thresher

The throbbing heart called you to task
and you answered,
you fed it,
spoon-wand,
vagabond

come to rest, to stroke
the hollow of my throat,
as I look up, and out—

Unentitled

Is it possible?
The latest occupant
of Stanford's stone pedestal,
another Rodin,
perches tentatively
above the library's turf,
half standing, half sitting
on her bronze rock, knee up.
A lesser known figure,
female, has taken over the heights.

She's not rooted
like the Thinker who mortar-and-pestles
fist against jawbone;
she doesn't thrust into space
like great-bellied Balzac.
Yet chiseled beneath her feet too
the word *Thinker* shadows the stone.
Can Rodin have imagined a woman
so full with thoughts of her own?

I've never had a statue
pay me less mind;
her eyes turned to the grass
are blurred, her lips
open as if to shape
what she sees.

Her upraised thigh, I admit,
claims as much of my attention.
The space it creates, a dancing triangle
bounded by thigh, calf, rock,
is the clearest shape

the figure offers.
It beckons me to circle,
looking up through it to glimpse
the rocky tuft of her crotch.

Why, even as she meditates,
must she pose so alluringly?
It's a position—half this, half that—
which no one would want to hold for long.

Let me look closer—
a small plaque
fixed to the old block reads
Whistler's Muse.

                Of course,
the Thinker's relocated,
his legend left in the stone.

Now I see why Rodin
cut her off at the biceps.

Whistle me up no armless muses,
I mutter to the evening air.

Still, she's out there
in the middle of the lawn,
where the sprinklers of Stanford burst out all around her.

Dense as mist beneath a waterfall,
the spray keeps two young men
from reading the small print. "*Thinker.*
There must be a whole series of them,"
says one, his cap bill-backwards.

stanza break

For the time being then,
the more-than-muse remains, a presence
whose effects I can't foresee.

The window-angle of her leg
now frames violet blue,
now the headlamp of an airplane
disappearing into her knee—
now whatever you, my friend, can find.

II

The Upstairs Room

Here at the top of the house,
this room's always waiting
for us to rise to its occasion.
A host of windows introduce the light,
which has changed since last we looked.
The north offers wide sky,
the east, the swirling crinolines of leaves.
A trellis to the south abstracts the out-of-doors:
each square's a pool of blue and green,
none like any other.
Each day becomes itself . . .

A mockingbird keeps making overtures.
And people next door, calling back and forth.
You've dashed off before the squirrels,
                                      I lie here still.

The ceiling billows upward
like the sheet you lofted, floating
for a long, light moment,
just now.

Happy Donuts

offers as much as you imagine:
frosted frilled embellished,
plumped and squirting jelly,
though none so fine

as the blown-up photos
with milk and berries,
or that aerial view of glistening
crullers in diagonal stripes,
flanking their corporal,
a bottomless well
of joe.

Formica,
teal, maroon, and gold,
comes to seem warm
as you settle in to read.

When at night fluorescence
flickers on, the ur-donut looms
suspended overhead—
eight feet across, shiny golden brown—
the mother ship.

The things I miss—
when they spring to light,
abashed awakenings!

Small mahogany horses cresting together in one wave
before a donut portrait

like saboteurs before the big screen,
dwarfed, but suddenly real.
Who chose these ornaments? These particular
dolphins leaping underneath the clock
as if it were the sun,
that Eiffel tower straddling the bubble milk tea,
another brushed against a painted sky—
a distant post a child could grasp
and swing around and off
to land, who knows—
ollyolly oxenfree . . .
                    Cambodia behind . . .

Yes, there's a bamboo silhouette
of Angkor Wat, the temple.
And two, no, three altars.

One's hidden, unless
you glimpse a reddish light
behind the counter, where
ancestral teacups gather
around a 10-watt candle.

Next, on a corner shelf
up high for you to find,
Buddha's entertained
with an apple-green apple
at one hand, at the other,
an apple-shaped jar
of apple juice.

Third, a graceful figurine
invites us to trade, honored
with incense (but who lit it,

who blew it out?),
a bottle of Crystal Geyser,
and a glazed old-fashioned—
fire, water, grain . . .

Curios—blessings—multiply,
especially the stuck-together families
of round-eyed china cats,
each holding up a paw,
Welcome! Always Open!

Lately I've learned
that one family, three brothers,
keep the donut haven:
Sam, the eldest,
Cheng, his wife, her talk like song
beneath the working thrum,
and their sprite, Kayli—
the tiny brass bells
on her ankles almost tell
where she's run to—
Jim, the quiet middle son,
who works the nights overflowing
with students and buffoons,
Jack who wants to know all about you,
and Orn, his bride—here at last!
spring weather in her smile—
a pig butcher before she threaded
her way through immigration,
surrendering love letters
into their skeptical hands.

two-line break

Today, the young father
makes flute-whistle noises
through his palms,
twiddling his fingers for a trill.
When the child can't do it too,
she yodels, crows it out.
Sam laughs. The anklets clink.
Kayli chins herself on a pastry case
and peeks at me through the glass,
her face, curiously round
among the many circles
that keep appearing,
always fresh.

On My Own

Night   no darker than
                              plums
     soft   as a fan's breath
    flows past
            the young orchestra

I also practice
            wandering

Avenues of lamps and branches
       meander too

The pine-chilled breeze fills me

with emptiness
                My feet
   ring with it

                    Flatfooted I
                       can't hurry yet I do
reeling in the paths
           my own
           to you

Jet Lagged in Oxford

We sleep overlapping
shifts in half light,
the bed (home!) a cloud-covered raft.

We've tumbled to it,
really two singles, a great rift
down the center—who are *we*
when we're at home?

Moored, unmoored, constrained
to drift in separate bunks,
or awaken, some morning,
wrenched . . .

Gamely nonetheless, you throw
your hodgepodge of limbs across,
not minding (my sweet) the gap.

The Stanford Quad as Evening Falls

Highly colored as a Bible pamphlet lacking
depth of field, a mural mounts over the chapel's
triple doors—Christ speaking to the masses,
surrounded by bits of Byzantine gilt.

Nonetheless, the compound with its dusty tan arcades
persists in looking Moorish, like some exotic movie set.
The backdrop—the sky—turns lavender at twilight.
Frowsy palms thrust into it,
towering over the sandcastles.

Displayed at the entrance—a collector's
coup—in carved rags and nooses
to ransom their neighbors,
Rodin's burghers give it all up.

The students passing by tell themselves,
"All that I can imagine is mine."

Yet in one earthquake after another,
the buildings, made of sand, fall apart.
The shock of a recent temblor
sent the pavement surging out in waves—
jouncing, bucking a girl on her bike
as glass globes of lanterns burst.

Tonight the sea of tiles is calm.
Two children run by, bare feet slapping
on the cat's tongue roughness of the brick.
Skateboards clatter up against the columns.

The crown of a palm tree tests the wind.

Coming Up with Questions

in the middle of the sidewalk
the enthusiasts of academe appear
with their tilted gestures
to say, things may come clear
if we look at them askew.
With a fine tension they stretch out their fingers
as far as they can, in as many directions,
then, seeming to catch some wisp,
curve them into a delicate clasp.
They caress their lips and faces with
the smooth knuckles of their tentative fists . . .
then snap them palm out like painted fans—
oh, the enameling is gorgeous, so tiny,
how it draws one in!

Anthropologist on Venus

The devotees stand on their toes,
feet cranked up on tiny slides
ending in what's called
the *toepiece*, a triangular vise
that forces the big toe
out of joint. Their heels
are strapped high
on attenuated shafts
called *stilettos*.
Gripped by this device,
we see from behind
the achievement
of each step—the wobble
and stab of it—
as the calf cramps,
a rocky bulge
the *desideratum*.
Many memorialize
this sacrifice
in what are called
thrillers: the craven pursuer
runs flat out, the pursued
demi-pointe, until
a grate, a root, catches
her up, the martyr
insensibly
shod.

At the Corner Table

Is he tucking away a gun, that guy
outside the plate-glass window?
Nonsense, I've never seen one
except snug on a cop,
or on *Homicide*—
that dynamite young man
I taught Shakespeare.
What an Antony, how fearful
with his cardboard blade!
Pistols crop up in the "cozies"
of course, whodunits
(with latte
at Happy Donuts).
The style, the eccentrics.
Most of all, the sleuth—
a friend, really . . .
The killer's just a fill-in,
the second smartest,
whose goat-eyes flash
at the climax—caught!
And the gun, merely a pretext,
a skeleton upon which hangs
delight—here amid
the newsprint . . . but, *was* he?
. . . the twenty-four-hour Ohs,
donuts with sprinkles
and toppling holes,
plugged out
by the dozen . . .

Building Down

"We're building down," my neighbor said.

      Gutting the basement
                              in surgical masks
they pry the plywood off—
          skreeling groans
                         as nails
              lose their grip—
bash the concrete back to rubble,
rend the fibrous trash,
and at last lay bare
              the stilts,
   too spindly
to keep on holding
                   the storied hulk . . .

Under hardwood:
      splinters, expired
          permits,
    crawl space
               black
     widow city.

                                      Flung out,
a rusted roller skate.

     Sandal-style like mine, at eight—

the magic
        of ball bearings—

stanza break

a footprint :
           telescoping,
                       with my own
skate key!

                   It's
not the where
            (up and down the block)

but the going—
     rush
          of motion and rust,
chattering over the cracks.

Presence

"The biggest bloom!
You can't see it—
shall I bring it in?"
Eric asks, arranging
bread and cheese.

With my foot up, waiting
for small bones to fuse,
I feel my years run short.

Tonight the Quakers
come to muse, concerning
how (or whether, one foot in)
we experience
leadings, perhaps
Light.

The circle settles into quiet.
Still I feel nerveless, spooked.
Alone with it.

Except for looking, the look of things . . .

The mauve rose, almost blown, opens out
beside the breadboard,
its short wick
lengthened by a wand of water.
Full of life now,
the rose gathers the room to itself.

Sewing Machine

Dark against the curtain-glow,
a horse arches, bends
to feed—rising as it reaches
down—a hummingbird
probes the silk.
What smaller, finer avian
rides on your back,
Singer of
the maker's joy,
unspooling as you go?

After the Ice Storm

It is a dream coming out on top, this
aberration of weather spun over the city.

When no one was attending,
freezing rain fused its layers thinner than petals;

everything grew thick and gleaming
with glacial clarity into the day.

Now you can smell the ice;
the curious cool takes you out

into the bulk of air,
fluid against your flown-open eyes.

Cars are locked to the ground by cloudy curves.
Dripping streams have bearded

the suspended traffic lights,
which go on beaming, red, then green,

over the waste. Houses melted to their hills,
right angles dissolve from the world.

And look, the municipal saplings
pruned to a minimal set of branches

have turned each so feverishly
singular!

stanza break

Everything is silent,
catching the light.

A tree bud,
resilient small pineapple

realized in cold,
seems to look back at you.

Reaching, you touch the ice-
found world, surface slicking off.

The Village Printing Shop
after a painting by Charles Ulrich

Grasping a cup, the apprentice
stands and drinks as if his sluicing throat,
fully drenched, could blossom—
like paper flowers that open out from pellets
to orchids: so grateful, nothing else matters,
not the congealing slick on the inkpot's
rim, the thwack and hist of trial sheets
around and off the press—
page by page by page—
too hot to touch.

At the Holocaust Museum
Washington, D.C.

1.

We wait for them to call our numbers
to enter the lift. *One fifty-eight* impels me
into a dull metal vault. It seals shut.
No buttons, no lighted markers.
We're ascending, I think. Then, nothing.
Finally the car opens—to vast darkness,
a journey from the upper story down.

2.

Suitcases, spectacles, supper pots—
belongings—wrenched
beside the train.

Here, a heap of scissors.
Toppled together,
splayed and corroding

they merge, a multitude
of mostly small ones—
sharp, snub-nosed, spindly,

some fashioned by hand.
Arbeit, wrought above the iron gate,
the taunt, *macht frei*.

3. Rabbi in a photo, Warsaw

He walks right at me,
listing in the wind as
his cane grinds
the pavement.

What a face, the hollows
dark as charcoal.
After each step,
another.

(Nearby on film, Goebbels exults
over a bonfire of books,
"hair-splitting intellectualism,"
consumed by flame.)

Despite his cane, the old man holds
four heavy volumes
against his ribs, on the heart side.
His beard rushes toward them.

His eyes,
more mild than fierce,
look at me as if to say,
You see?

4.

What haven't I said?
What of the literary motives,
worse, the excitement
I withheld at the checkroom,

where the woman with a lined face
handed me, silence for silence,
a cardboard circle ringed with metal.
But then, this place isn't about me.

I can't exchange looks with the rabbi
who seems to question me,
much less the village wives
and husbands-to-be, down a wall,

through a gap, and out of sight.
There's no one here to whom
I can begin to say
I am thee—

only who would I be without
such wielders of shears, delicate and blunt,
insisters upon perpetual questions—
makers, thinkers—

designers of this unwindowed space,
this journey to encounter
(thankful for my body's aching)
multitudes, belongings . . .

stanza break

and then return
the circle edged with metal,
shoulder my bookbag in the lobby,
and emerge into the traffic, the belated
                              afternoon light.

Grace among the Cacti
for Grace Estep Bloom, 1924-94

A particular woman,
Nevadan by way of
Carolina, she knew

what she wanted:
books, books! and
this bachelor, this well-

traveled lawyer,
hard at work like her
in Austria, the aftermath—

a Jew besides—
"dark" for the South.
She took to him,

reached across
the soft laps of Vienna
and told him so.

Grace and Norman
Nick-and-Nora'd all over
Europe, Israel,

lighting at last in Carson City,
their children the dazzled
niece and nephews, who read

stanza break

the books she edited
and later wrote,
on minerals and stars.

And then, just Grace.
Widowed at fifty-some
she woke, it had come

to this quarry—
harsh light,
cacti in skimpy pots.

She just . . .
let them be.
Drank, those nights.

Went on, did what she liked.
Clerked at the library,
paid them so she could.

Weekends, the Nugget—
with brunch you get a roll
of nickels—

one for the slots, and sprightly
clinked in her palm
out to the car

the other nineteen,
her adventure egg,
plus maybe a golden

stanza break

promotional pen
to mark
her maps with.

Grace, Gracie, sister of Annie,
Aunt Grace, how
she listened: the spark

to find out,
the quirk
to contradict . . .

On every step, stacks of books—
Forster, Sayers, Arendt—
borrowed, dwelt with, shared around,

and on display, the wire-rims
she'd plucked from mountain grass—
the Alps with Norman—spectacles

that "might have been Goethe's."

Behind the Windshield, 2003

Violets around Baghdad
 highlighted the uncertainty . . .

. . . Oh
 heard it wrong

allergic to the radio

Violets
 don't grow in Baghdad

They need water they're
 fragile

Pictures in the Firestorm

1.

Under this boy's fist, the dark
line of a marker rolls out—
no time to think—
a brontostegosaurus looms
over a shrunken tyrannosaur,
who stands accused, staring
at the monster's middle.
Large and small,
they lash their tails.
Above them the boy
outlines a rainbow and
only fills in the blues.

Clean sheet. A square
apartment block.
The small tyrannosaurus
stands tentatively at the door.
Tailless now, his orange outline
is rather like a person's,
even the horsy profile,
its undecided expression.
Is he knocking?
Or inside, hands against the pane?
A billboard with an arrow
pointing at the house proclaims,
NO ON LOVE.

stanza break

Page three, presto chango:
the looming dinosaur becomes
a dragon—red with rainbow razor scales.
Down on the now shrunken building
he launches a blast of flame.
Brilliant sun shines on him,
for he's the one,
the only one,
the only one to be.

2.

The poem like the boy
does not want
to make polite suggestions.
It wants to blurt that
NO ON LOVE
comes from the garrison
where we live.

Just outside,
or inside, a boy
hesitates, spring-loaded
at the threshold.

The house votes no on love.
The boy, one of many,
gives as good as he gets.
And then some.
And then some.

3.

Another vision begins with water.
Musing over the page, a girl
strokes the cool across the smooth,
then sketches green and purple
in the sea. Is it the same sea
as the boy's, his horizon,
where hydras block the harbor?
Here below the surface,
a mer-child stretches wide her wings,
to say, these are my friends.
A rooster holds forth
to an electrified eel,
a hummingbird swills
a blossom, and all
through the submerged castle,
butterflies float like astronauts.

4. *A riddle*

—Who would be invited
to an uncharted place
so full of light and space
it's almost not there?

—Those who fly, those who swim,
and those who feel their way
among them, finding kin.

5.

Thus, when Urashima
threw back the turtle he'd caught,
declaring, "I won't keep this old fellow
from all the dinners he has to come,"
the creature turned into a princess,
then took the gentle man
down to her palace in the deep.
He found that he could breathe just fine.
Of course, this joyful outcome's
not the end,
but it might have been.
Except for the lustrous box
Urashima forgot
not to open.

6.

Back in time,
he stood on the shore.
Many had died.

7.

Things happen so fast.
Sleek ballistics
and housings jack built,
hawked at trade shows
where the sand already burns,
dropped in squadrons
like wounded geese

by pilots on high, on auto,
high on the rush, the knife edge
of pure skill.

8.

After the strategic maps,
a single, late paragraph.

Turtle Saves Swimmer
Eleven miles off Brazil's coast, a man
whose boat capsized found himself
buoyed up by a sea-going turtle and
ferried to the shore. "It set him down
gentle—just like a parcel," a tourist who
saw the rescue remarked.

9.

A friend, snorkeling in September,
stills her delicious motion
to watch a group of sea turtles
steer and coast,
together, apart, the child
knocking within her inner sound,

then surfaces, to hear
that men have rammed and flamed
their planes against buildings
a hundred windows high—
plants on sills,

the dying, the terrified,
the no longer—

and wonders, why be human?
Why deliver a child to this—
why not a sea turtle, beyond
accounts of hate?

10.

The old portfolio—
that dragon boy,
that girl submerged,

a threshold with two faces,
welcome/obliteration.

And always a chorus milling around,
those who smile as they lament,
nature, nature.

His and hers—that's no answer,
certainly not for my friend
lifting her head above the waves.

Later in the lamplight, each of us
seems to ask, not why, but how—
how shall we be human?

Like water and breath, the asking.

2001, 2003-05

Perhaps a Glimpse

The way winter absolves the trees of foliage,
the way, especially at night, it picks out a denuded bush
that in summer punctuated a stretch of lawn with common bloom
and reveals it too as a tree, the brief trunk
a braid of roots untwirling into reaches
of sinew and praise,

the way the spindly branches hold up like ornaments
a few brownpapery clusters of blossom,
each piled with snow, precarious,
but there's no wind now—

Gandhi, of course—the bare limbs,
the shadow long uphill.

To be harmed, and not . . .

I can hardly say it.

At least, then, to stand here
a little longer.

              It's cold,
and still,
      how lightly the grains of snow
trace the contours of the bark, the fractured
walk, the rising and falling ground.

Notes

Sight Unseen. The acute accent on Ácoma, while not conventional, is included to indicate stress on the syllable.

Making a Scene. Andre Braugher is a screen, stage, and television actor who won an Obie award for the title role in Shakespeare's *Henry V* and an Emmy for his role as Detective Frank Pembleton in the TV series *Homicide: Life on the Street.*

The Stanford Quad as Evening Falls. Rodin's *The Burghers of Calais* portrays the surrender of six eminent men in 1347 to Edward III of England, who offered to spare their besieged town in return for their lives. Rodin's monument shows the men as they deliver the keys to the city, barely clothed and prepared to die.

At the Corner Table. For Lisa Steinman. A "cozy," named after the tea cozy, is a pleasant murder mystery with a quaint setting, typically a village or country house in England.

Presence. The italicized line comes from Walt Whitman.

The Village Printing Shop. The painting with the same title by Charles Frederick Ulrich (1884) is in the Musée d'Art Américain, Terra Foundation for the Arts, Giverny, France.

At the Holocaust Museum. *Arbeit macht frei:* Work makes you free. The photograph that section three describes is by Roman Vishniac.

Grace among the Cacti. *Nick-and-Nora'd:* Nick and Nora Charles are the sophisticated, adventurous, delightedly married sleuths in the *Thin Man* film series of the nineteen thirties and forties based on a novel by Dashiell Hammet.

Pictures in the Firestorm. The Japanese story of Urashima and the quotation in section five are adapted from Joanna Cole's *Best-Loved Folktales of the World* (Anchor-Doubleday, 1982). The images in section seven are inspired by three documentary films: *Hearts and Minds* (1974); *Hidden Wars of Desert Storm* (2000); and *Who's Counting* (1995), based on the book *If Women Counted* (1988) by Marilyn Waring, former Minister of Parliament of New Zealand.

About the Author

Photograph by Renée Burgard

Lauren Rusk teaches at Stanford University and spends parts of each year in Portland, Oregon, and Oxford, England. She has also published a study of autobiographical prose, *The Life Writing of Otherness: Woolf, Baldwin, Kingston, and Winterson.*

www.ingramcontent.com/pod-product-compliance
Lightning Source LLC
Chambersburg PA
CBHW052113070526
44584CB00017B/2464